CLASSIC \ ∕ ∪

Today's Questions. Timeless Answers.

Looking for time-tested guidance for the dilemmas of the spiritual life? Find it in the company of the wise spiritual masters of our Catholic tradition.

Comfort in Hardship: Wisdom from Thérèse of Lisieux

Inner Peace: Wisdom from Jean-Pierre de Caussade

Life's Purpose: Wisdom from John Henry Newman

Path of Holiness: Wisdom from Catherine of Siena

Secrets of the Spirit: Wisdom from Luis Martinez

A Simple Life: Wisdom from Jane Frances de Chantal

Solace in Suffering: Wisdom from Thomas à Kempis

Strength in Darkness: Wisdom from John of the Cross

Forthcoming volumes will include wisdom from:
Francis de Sales
James Alberione

Path of Holiness

CLASSIC WISDOM COLLECTION

Path of Holiness

Wisdom from Catherine of Siena

Edited and with a Foreword by Mary Lea Hill, FSP

Pauline
BOOKS & MEDIA
Boston

Library of Congress Cataloging-in-Publication Data

Catherine, of Siena, Saint, 1347-1380.
  [Correspondence. English. Selections]
  Path of holiness : wisdom from Catherine of Siena / edited and with a foreword
by Mary Lea Hill.
      p. cm. -- (Catholic wisdom collection)
  Selections from the author's correspondence and Dialogue.
  Includes bibliographical references (p. 97).
  ISBN 0-8198-5963-X (pbk.)
  1. Catherine, of Siena, Saint, 1347-1380-- Correspondence. I. Hill, Mary Lea. II.
Catherine, of Siena, Saint, 1347-1380. Libro della divina dottrina. English.
Selections. III. Title. IV. Series.
  BX4700.C4A4 2011
  282.092--dc22

                          2010043346

The Scripture quotations contained herein are from the *New Revised Standard Version Bible: Catholic Edition*, copyright © 1989, 1993, Division of Christian Education of the National Council of the Churches of Christ in the United States of America. Used by permission. All rights reserved.

Other Scripture references are translated from Catherine of Siena's own wording of the text as she dictated to her followers.

Cover design by Rosana Usselmann

Cover photo by Mary Louise Winters, FSP

"P" and PAULINE are registered trademarks of the Daughters of St. Paul.

Published by Pauline Books & Media, 50 Saint Pauls Avenue, Boston, MA 02130-3491

Printed in the U.S.A.

www.pauline.org

Pauline Books & Media is the publishing house of the Daughters of St. Paul, an international congregation of women religious serving the Church with the communications media.

1 2 3 4 5 6 7 8 9 10   16 15 14 13 12 11

For all the strong women
I have known—
in gratitude for
their witness to Christ

Contents

Foreword

As we novices settled into our rooms at the retreat house, I noted aloud, "This is pretty ascetical, isn't it?" We were studying ascetical theology at that time and just beginning to dabble in some real-life applications. Forty-some years later, I can confirm my note: That place was *very* ascetical. It had formerly been the seminary of some very hearty missionaries and comprised an austere series of small farmhouses and a converted horse stable: hot, musty, and infested. The good seminarians kept the old buildings together rather nicely by foreign mission standards, but we city girls had never seen a convenience we didn't like. Besides spiders and bats, plenty of mosquitoes buzzed around, headquartered in the Concord River below our property. Ah, yes, night prayer outside beneath the trees was second only to human sacrifice. Each mosquito seemed bent on consuming another being a million times bigger than itself.

This experience was my youthful version of true sacrifice. I did try to "offer it up," not that God wasn't up there chuckling at the whole scene. But to me, the rest of life wasn't much of a sacrifice. Retreat experiences were the extraordinary. However, I had become enthralled with someone who did make real sacrifices, and who did so willingly and even joyfully: Saint Catherine of Siena.

One of the mainstays of community entertainment in those days was an old Italian film on Catherine's life. It was a black and white wonder, jumping and scratching its way through the projector. Today's critics might consider it tacky, but it succeeded in dramatizing many of Catherine's internal joys and struggles. One of my favorite scenes was of wild horses racing around in her tiny cell. Their fury did some justice to the inner turmoil and temptations carnival revelers caused from outside.[1]

After watching the film, I launched into a marvelous biography of Saint Catherine written by Johannes Jorgensen. He traced her steps from her earliest days in Siena, Italy, to her premature death thirty-three years later. Jorgensen helped me see the reality of Catherine. I could sense her apprehension in the face of her calling, her wonder at the trust God placed in her, her bold confidence before princes and popes, her maternal love for her disciples and co-workers, her internalizing of every struggle and pain of the Church. From this saint, I learned about the personal nature of a religious vocation, how within a calling there is a particular relationship and responsibility. Many people receive the call to spend a lifetime in the company of Jesus Christ, but Jesus calls each one to a unique expression, an individual *yes* that will mold that person into a singular saintliness.

The singular holiness of Catherine Benincasa (1347–1380) manifested itself in her early childhood. The six-year-old Catherine first encountered Jesus Christ while on an errand with her brother, Stefano, when Jesus appeared to her above the Church of Saint Dominic accompanied by saints Peter, Paul, and John the Evangelist. Jesus was seated on a throne, dressed in priestly garments, and wearing a pope's crown. He said nothing to the little girl but simply gave her a blessing. However, in that encounter, Jesus captured her heart and her imagination.

Catherine soon dedicated her virginity to God, and as the years progressed, she turned down many marriage proposals, much to her parents' dismay. Thinking she was in the midst of some youthful fantasy, they loaded her with household duties. But Catherine's love of God was very real and deep, and her family eventually recognized the presence of something extraordinary in this young woman, so caught up in prayer. To fulfill her desire to fully dedicate herself to God, Catherine joined the Sisters of Penance of Saint Dominic, a secular religious group known as the Mantallate[2] because of the heavy Dominican capes they wore. These sisters lived independently but gathered for daily Mass and prayer. During her early years as a Mantallata, Catherine practiced many penances, including reducing to a minimum her intake of food and her sleep. In 1370, in the midst of her mystical experiences, Catherine received the stigmata, although the marks remained invisible. A few months later, she suddenly fell into a state similar to death in which she heard Jesus admonish her to awaken so that he might send her on a mission to popes and rulers and to the whole Church.

Upon awakening, Catherine embarked on numerous trips, first to convince the Pope to return to Rome from Avignon, France, but also to mediate peace between the warring cities of Italy. Catherine's extensive travel undoubtedly brought hardships. Aside from the physical sufferings, Catherine was often rebuffed as proud and delusional because of her apostolic audacity. She was accused of scandalous behavior because she was accompanied by many young men and women, as well as by numerous clerics. However, Catherine, known to her followers as "Mama," was preparing these companions so that after her death they could continue her work of reform.

Her writings are her lasting gifts to us. Besides *The Dialogue,* which recounts her mystical conversations with God the Father, we have a collection of prayers and some 400 letters written to family, friends, popes, kings, queens, city officials, and many other notable persons involved in the historical drama of that day. Through Catherine's untiring efforts, Pope Gregory XI returned to Rome in 1376, although discord and wars continued almost unabated.[3] All of this turmoil weighed on Catherine's heart. By 1380, the burden Christ gave to her became too heavy, and she fell to the ground as if crushed by its weight, which she thought of as the ship of the Church. Two months later, after advising her followers about the path they should take with their lives, she died at the age of thirty-three, calling out to the Blood of Christ for mercy upon the Church. In recognition for her mission on behalf of the Church, she has been declared both a doctor of the Church and a patroness of Europe.[4]

I think often of those days when I was a willing "Caterinati"—when I was new in religious life and penances could still be made up, and the reasons for them were mostly dreams. Yet, as time moves on and our lives fill out, we find many occasions of penance. For the most part these sacrifices involve drudgery and disappointment, but sometimes more acute suffering is sprinkled in. Catherine would not want us to waste any of those moments.

She was not a morose saint, concentrating too much on suffering and on hopes of martyrdom. She was a mystic very much in tune with the sufferings Christ offered for our salvation. Great mystics are few. God chooses them to give or to receive his message for a particular time in history, setting them as mirrors before the rest of us. In Catherine's person, the great ones of her day should have been able to see the face of Christ and hear his word.

In our day, Catherine's legacy gives us a glimpse of the divine dealings with our souls. She has dictated in her *Dialogue* and in her letters a clear commentary on Christian love. God the Father expects us to put on, as clothing, the example of his Son. He explains that what we would like to do out of love for him we must instead do for others. He may ask us to carry out our works of charity under the most normal circumstances, or he may ask us to love in some very difficult situations.

God entrusted to Catherine a message of reform. He wanted not only the great events affecting society reformed in the light of Christ, but also the small events of each personal life. We can reform our world and ourselves in Christ through our attitudes toward persons and events. Our life of penance can simply be the effort to be a loving person, to absorb any negative energy we encounter, and to permeate the world around us with the energy of Christ.

Like Saint Paul, Catherine counted on the power of her own weakness. She knew that God is easily won by a humble spirit. Yet like the great apostle, she knew how to find strength in weakness. She presented what had to be done in the life of the Church and in the lives of individuals as something "God wills and *I* will for you." Perhaps we do not feel the same certainty as Catherine, but she is God's sign for us that he does will our sanctification, and that by our holiness we are to "up the ante" for the Church and the world. We need not worry about whether we are pleasing God or just fooling ourselves. We will see clearly, as in a mirror, the perfection of charity to which we are called.

I

On Moderation

I, Catherine, your poor unworthy mother, want you to attain that perfection for which God has chosen you. It appears to me that if someone desired this perfection, she would always proceed with moderation, and never without it. Every work would be done both with moderation *and* without it, for the proper way to love God is without moderation, without limit, measure, or rule. Love for him should be without measure. If you desire perfect love, that desire must also organize your life. Your first rule should be to turn from every human conversation that is only conversation, unless charity demands differently. Love people very much, but talk with only a few of them. Learn to talk little, even with those you love in a spiritual manner. Remember that unless you do this you are limiting the love you owe to God without even realizing it. You are placing a finite creature between yourself and God. In other words, you are giving a creature the love you should give to God. You delay your own perfection by this immoderate love of a creature. Instead, have a love that is spiritual and disciplined.

— Excerpt from an undated letter written
to Monna Alessa Dei Saracini, a Mantallata

II

Faith Comes from Love

I beg you, dearest father, to fervently pray that both of us may drown in the humble Lamb's blood, which will surely make us strong and faithful. We will feel the burning fire of divine love and be co-workers with his grace, and not despoilers or destroyers of it. In this way we witness our fidelity to God, our trust in him, rather than our own sufficiency or our trust in anyone else.

It is with this same faith that we will love a creature, for just as love of neighbor comes from our love of God, so does faith, both in general and in particular. For as there is a general faith that corresponds to the love we feel toward all creatures, so there is a special faith between those whose mutual love is closer. This latter is like the more particular love that exists between the two of us, a love demonstrated by our faith. So much love is manifested that it is impossible to imagine that either of us desires anything but the other's good. It is an earnest belief because it insists both in the sight of God and of men that what is sought in the other is solely the glory of God's name and the good of the soul. And we beg God himself to provide, along with burdens, an increase of fortitude and perseverance. This kind of faith sustains the one who loves, never letting that love waver for any reason, whether from the tongue of man or the wiles of the devil, or even because of distance. If anyone should do differently, it shows that love of God and neighbor is imperfect.

— Excerpt from an undated letter written to Brother Raymond of Capua, OP, Catherine's confessor and biographer

III

Pursuing God Alone

Often a soul that sees it has progressed by means of some great penance wishes to have all people proceed the same way, and is shocked and displeased if they do not, as if they have done wrong. But perhaps that one is actually making more progress and is more virtuous than the one criticizing him, even without doing as much penance. Perfection does not consist in punishing the body or killing it, but in killing our perverse self-will. This is the way we should desire all to walk, submitting our will to the sweet will of God. Penance and bodily discipline is good, but they are not the rule for everyone, since all bodies are not alike. Often one has to give up the penance begun because something unforeseen happens. If we, then, built our spiritual foundation on penance, or encouraged others to do so, we may find we have nothing, and worse yet, find ourselves so imperfect that even consolation and virtue fail us. The reason for this is that when the thing we set our heart on and made so central disappears, we feel that God has disappeared and we fall victim to despondency, becoming sad and bitter; this in turn deprives us of the fervent, active prayer we used to experience. You see, then, what misfortune would befall you if you concentrate solely on penance. Ignorance, criticism, weariness, and a bitter spirit would result if all your effort was in providing God with a finished work, when he who is infinite Good only requires infinite desire of us. We should concentrate instead on killing and destroying our bad will so that we can place it before God as the loving, eager, infinite desire for his glory and the salvation of souls. We will find nourishment at the table of holy desire where there is nothing offensive, either from self or from another, but only joy and goodness. What a miserable woman I am! I regret that I never lived out the truth of this teaching; no, I did just the opposite and so I feel that I have often been irritable and judgmental toward my neighbor. By the love of Christ crucified, I hope to find healing for this and all my other infirmities so that today we together can set out on the way of truth, inspired to build a right foundation on holy intentions, not relying on mere appearances and impressions. This will help us avoid self-neglect and judgment of other's faults, except out of compassion or as a general correction.

— Excerpt from an undated letter written to Sister Daniella of Orvieto, a Dominican nun

IV

Spiritual Practices

The soul obtains every grace and virtue by self-knowledge, as we have said. Where else does a soul find
such a rich sorrow for sin or the abundance of God's mercy,
if not in this self-knowledge? Do we possess it or not? Let
us see. In your letter you wrote that despite your desire to
experience true contrition for your sins, you feel no sorrow and so you refrain from receiving Holy Communion.
Is this what you should do? You know how good God is
and that he loved you before you were born. As the eternal
wisdom his power over virtue is immeasurable. And so, he
certainly has the power, wisdom, and desire to give us

whatever we need. He actually gives us even more than we ask for, more than we could ever dream of seeking. Did we ask to be created as intelligent beings, made in his own image and likeness, rather than as simple, unintelligent beasts? Certainly not.

I also hear from you: "I believe all that you say about him, but why is it that even when I ask for something like sorrow for my sins, I don't receive it?" Here is my answer: The difficulty could certainly be with the person who asks, perhaps imprudently, only speaking the words, but not being wholeheartedly engaged. Of such people, our Savior said that they call out, "Lord, Lord," hoping to be acknowledged by him (see Mt 7:21). It is not that he does not know them, but his mercy does not recognize them because of their faults.

Perhaps you prayed for something that would prove detrimental to salvation. Some ask for what they do not seem to have, but they do in fact have it. We only ask for what we imagine will benefit us, but actually it might prove harmful. Since it is actually better for us not to have it, God has satisfied the intention for which it was asked. From God's perspective, we have to say that our prayer is always answered.

. . . Now I would like to speak about the attitude we should have toward Holy Communion and what benefit comes to us from receiving it. Foolish humility, such as that which some men have toward the secular world, should be avoided. Instead I tell you that we should receive the sweet sacrament because it is the food of souls and we cannot live a life of grace without it. Nothing is so important, no bond so great that it should keep us away from this sweet sacrament. Each of us should do as much as we can on our own part, and it will be sufficient. How should we receive it? With the light of holy faith, and with the mouth of holy desire. In the light of faith we are able to contemplate the true God and true Man present in the Host. After seeing this intellectually, we receive the Host tenderly and with a holy meditation on our sins and faults, in order to arrive at true sorrow and a consideration for God who with such generous and immeasurable love gives himself to us as food. Let us not turn away because we do not have the perfect contrition or the disposition of heart that we wish we had; simply having good will is sufficient and it is something we can easily obtain.

. . . I have said that it is unbecoming, and I do not want you to do as many imprudent men do, that is, to ignore what the Holy Church commands them, saying: "I am unworthy of it." Because of this, they spend extensive time in mortal sin deprived of the food of their souls. What foolishness! It is obvious to everyone that you are unworthy. When are you expecting this worthiness? Do not waste your time, for in the end you will be no more worthy than you are now. Not even with all of our good works could we ever be worthy. It is from God, who is worthy, that we take on worthiness. His worth never lessens. What then should we do? Let us make ourselves ready by observing his loving commandment. For if we do not do so, and give up Communion, thinking this will help us flee from fault, we would actually fall into fault.

Therefore let me conclude by saying that I do not want this kind of foolishness in you. Rather, prepare yourself well, as a faithful Christian, to receive Holy Communion. You will receive it as perfectly as you know yourself and not otherwise. Living in that knowledge will help you to see clearly. Do not weaken your resolve even in the face of pain or loss, injury or ingratitude, even if from those you have served; but courageously, with sincere endurance, you should persevere until death. This is what I implore you, by the love of Christ crucified, to do. I say nothing more. Remain in the holy and sweet grace of God. Sweet Jesus, Jesus love.

— Excerpt from an undated letter written to
Messer Ristoro Canigiani, a pious layman of Florence

V

On Love of God

Without expecting any advantage for himself, God gave us the Word, his only-begotten Son. Truly, we provide him no profit. In our case it is different because even though we have nothing to offer him, we ourselves do profit. While the flower of honor is his, the fruit of profit is ours. He has loved us without being loved, and we love because we are loved. He loves us because of grace, and we love him because of duty, because we are bound to love him. It is impossible for us to bring any profit to God any more than we can love him because of grace, aside from duty. It is we who are bound to him, and not he to us, because before he was loved, he loved us and created us in his image and likeness. And so, there it is: We are neither capable of being profitable to him, nor capable of loving him with this kind of first love. God does require that we love him as he loved us without any second thoughts. How are we to do this, then, since he asks something of us of which we are incapable? We can do it because he has given us the means to love him freely, not expecting any profit to ourselves: We can be useful to our neighbor. So this is the means we have to obey what he asks of us for the glory and praise of his name and to show him our love: We must give service and love to every human being, opening up our love to the good and the bad, to every kind of people, to those who are kind to us and to those who criticize us. We believe that God is not influenced by persons, but by holy desires, and that his love reaches out to the just and to sinners. For God is no respecter of persons, but of holy desires, and his charity extends over the just and sinners.

— Excerpt from an undated letter written to
Brother Matteo Di Francesco Tolomei, OP

VI

On Love of Neighbor

We ought to be servants because we are bought with his blood. However, I do not see how our service can be profitable to him; therefore, we should be of profit to our neighbor, because the neighbor is the means by which we test and gain virtue. You know that every virtue receives life from love, and love is gained in love, that is, by raising the eye of our mind to behold how much we are beloved of God. Seeing ourselves loved, we cannot do otherwise than love. Loving him, we shall embrace virtue through the force of love, and shall hate vice and turn from it.

So you see that we conceive virtues through God, and bring them to birth for our neighbor. You are well aware that for the needs of your neighbor you bring forth the child charity from your soul, along with patience with whatever wrongs your neighbor does to you. You pray, especially for those who have done you wrong. And this we should do; even if people are untrue to us, we should be true to them, and faithfully seek their salvation; loving them by grace, and not for personal gain. In other words, do not love your neighbor for your own profit, for that would not be faithful love, and you would not be responding to the love God has for you. For as God has loved you by grace, so he wills that since you are unable to return this love to him, you return it to your neighbor, loving him by grace and not, as I already pointed out, as part of a deal. So whether you are wronged or should see that love is withheld or your joy is lessened, you must not be stingy or withhold love toward your neighbor. Instead you should love him tenderly, bear with and endure his faults. Always be reverent toward God's servants and find consolation in them.

Take care not to behave like mad or foolish people who pretend to investigate and judge the actions and habits of God's servants. Anyone who acts this way deserves a severe rebuke. This would be the same as trying to rein in the Holy Spirit as if we could make all the servants of God walk in our own way—an impossible feat to achieve.

— Excerpt from an undated letter written to Caterina Di Scetto, a Mantellata

VII

Embracing Suffering

Indeed, this is the truth, sweetest mother, that if you love my soul more than my body, you will find consolation and not be so troubled. I would like you to learn from our sweet Mother Mary, who for God's honor and our salvation, gave us her dead Son upon the wood of the Cross. After Christ ascended into heaven and Mary was left alone, she lived with his holy disciples. Mary and those disciples consoled one another greatly. Although it would be a great sorrow to part, she consented, for the sake of her Son's glory and praise and the good of the whole world, and they departed. She chose the sorrow of their parting rather than the consolation of their remaining, solely because of the love she possessed for God's honor and our salvation. Now, dearest mother, I want you to learn from her example. You know that I must follow God's will, and I know that you also want me to follow it. His will has been that I go away, and this has not happened without some mystery, nor without very valuable fruit. It was his will that I come here, not the decision of any other person. Whatever else is said, it is not the truth. And so, it is best for me to continue following his footsteps, however and whenever it please his immeasurable goodness. As a good, sweet mother, you must not be disturbed, but be content and accept every suffering for God's honor and for the salvation of both of us. Recall that you did this very same thing for this world's gain, when your sons left you to seek temporal riches. Now, for the sake of eternal life, it seems to be such a burden to you that you threaten to run away if I do not reply quickly. All this, because you have more love for that part of me which I received from you—that is, your flesh, with which you clothed me—than for the part I received from God. So now, lift up your heart and your mind to the sweet and holy cross where all suffering ends. Willingly take a little of this world's pain in order to escape the eternal pain we merit by our sins. Be consoled for the love of Christ crucified. You have not been abandoned by

God or by me. You will indeed be comforted and completely consoled. Just think that the suffering has not been so great that the joy will not be greater.

— Excerpt from a letter written to
Monna Lapa Benincasa, Catherine's mother, 1376

VIII

Willingness to Sacrifice

How blind is the sick man who does not know his own need, and blind the shepherd-physician, who is concerned with nothing but pleasing and having an advantage. This is obviously his intention, because he refuses to use the knife of justice or the fire of ardent charity! Such men illustrate Christ's words: If one blind man guides another, both will fall into the ditch (see Lk 6:39). The sick man and the physician fall into hell. Such a man is indeed a hired hand, not a shepherd, for he does not yank his sheep away from the wolf, but devours them himself (see Jn 10:7–18). And what is the reason for this? It is because he loves himself instead of God. He is not a follower of our sweet Jesus, the true shepherd, who has given his life for his sheep. We see, then, how dangerous this type of love is for ourselves and for others. It is to be avoided because of the great harm it can bring to many people. I pray that by God's goodness, my venerable Father, you will extinguish this in yourself, and not love yourself for your own sake, nor your neighbor for yourself, nor even God; but that you will love him because he is our highest and eternal Good, worthy of our love. Love yourself and your neighbor for the honor and glory of the sweet name of Jesus. I will this: that you be so good and true a shepherd that if you had a hundred thousand lives you would willingly give all of them for God's honor and the salvation of souls.

— Excerpt from a letter written to Pope Gregory XI, 1375

IX

The Soul Filled with Virtue

If a soul was enlightened by discretion, that soul would know that nothing except the lack of virtues can deprive it of God. It possesses eternal life because of virtue through the Blood of Christ. So let us rise above every imperfection and set our attention on those true virtues, which are so splendid and beautiful that they cannot be fully described.

No one can trouble the soul founded on virtue, or deprive it of the hope of heaven. This person has put self-will to death in all things, spiritual as well as temporal. The heart is not set on penance, personal consolations, or private revelations, but on persevering in love of virtue through

Christ crucified. Because of this, it is patient, faithful, hopeful in God and not in itself or its works, humble and obedient, and believes others rather than itself. In other words, it is not presumptuous. It opens its arms wide in mercy and so dispels confusion of mind. Amid doubt and conflict it raises the light of faith, and works courageously with true and profound humility. With joyfulness it enters within itself, not allowing the heart to become giddy. It is strong and it perseveres because it put to death that which made it weak and ineffectual, its own will. It is always the right time and the right place for this soul. During the penitential season, it enjoys a time of gladness and consolation because it uses penance the right way, as a means. If, by some necessity or for obedience, penance has to be abandoned, the soul rejoices because it is founded in the love of virtue that cannot be taken away, nor is it. It recognizes that any contradiction offered by the will must be strongly and diligently resisted.

— Excerpt from an undated letter written to
Sister Daniella of Orvieto, a Dominican nun

X

On Reconciliation

Observe the teaching that our crucified Master gives you: It is the one thing that my soul most desires to see in you, that is, love and affection for your neighbor, with whom you have been at war for so long. You yourself know that the tree of your soul will dry up and not bear fruit without this root of love. If you continue with this hate it will be unable to drink any of the needed moisture of grace. Remember, dearest father, that the sweet First Truth teaches this to you, and has given the commandment to love God above everything, and one's neighbor as one's self. You have the Lord's own example of hanging upon the wood of the most holy cross. When his enemies cried: "Crucify him!" (Lk 23:21) he called out meekly and gently: "Father, forgive them; for they do not know what they are doing" (Lk 23:34). Observe carefully his mysterious love! He does not only pardon them, but also excuses them before his Father! This is such an important example and teaching for us, that the just one, who has none of the poison of sin, suffers from the unjust the punishment of our sins!

Therefore I beg you, and it is my will that you follow Christ crucified, and show love for your neighbor's salvation. By this you will prove that you follow the Lamb, with his same burning desire for his Father's honor and the salvation of souls. He chose bodily death and so should you, my lord! Do not be distressed if you lose your worldly treasure; such loss will be your gain if you reconcile with your brother. I am amazed that you are not willing to devote your temporal means to this, and, if necessary, your life as well, considering the great destruction there has been to both souls and bodies, and how many religious, women, and children have been injured or exiled during this war. No more, for the love of Christ crucified!

— Excerpt from an undated letter written to
Charles V, King of France

XI

Living a Christian Life

I desire to see you constant and persevering in virtue, for it is not the one who begins who is crowned, but only the one who perseveres. For perseverance is the reigning queen who stands between fortitude and true patience, but she alone wears the crown of glory. So I want you to be constant and persevering in virtue, dearest brother, that you may be rewarded for your work. I hope in the great goodness of God that he will strengthen you in this way so that neither the demon nor your fellow man can cause you to go backward.

According to your letter, you have begun well. Your desire to work for your salvation makes me rejoice very much. You start by saying that you have forgiven everyone who wronged you or who wished you harm. How necessary this is when you want to have God fill your soul with grace, and to be at peace with the world. The one who harbors hate is deprived of God and is as if already condemned, living a foretaste of hell, for he is devouring himself, seeking revenge and living in fear. Such a person presumes to slay his enemy but actually kills himself, for his soul is slain with the knife of hate. On the other hand, one who truly forgives through the love of Christ crucified, has peace and quiet, and is not disturbed. Every bit of anger in his soul has been slain, and God who rewards every good, gives him the grace of eternal life at the end. How happy that soul will be then! No one can describe its joy or its peace of conscience. Even the world accords great honor to one who for love of virtue and generosity avoids the desire to seek payback from his enemy. So I invite you to find consolation as you persevere in this holy resolution.

With good conscience you can insist on what is rightfully yours, if you do so in a reasonable manner. No one is obliged to relinquish more than he wants to give up; however, one who freely abandons his possessions will reach a higher perfection. It is advisable not to go to the bishop's house or to the palace, but to stay at home in peace. For we are weak, and in the presence of notable people we find our own soul excited. We may do unjust or foolish things to show that we know more than someone else, or because of greed. It is much better to avoid these places.

But here is another thing: When poor men and women who are clearly in the right, but who need assistance, reveal to us the reason why they have no money, God would be honored if you were to take up their cause. Do this out of charity, like Saint Ives, who was the lawyer of the poor in his time. To show pity to the poor and care for their needs with the abilities God has given you is indeed pleasing to God and will be meritorious for your own salvation. . . .

Ask pardon fully of everyone, so that with your neighbor you will always have the joy of charity. And, dearest brother, about selling the goods that you have over and above what you need, and the expensive clothes, you do well to try to remedy this. (Such clothes are very harmful and can fill your heart with vanity and nourish it with pride, since these things make a man appear more important, and encourage boasting. What a disgrace to see our head in torment while we allow ourselves such luxuries. Saint Bernard said it is not right for the limbs of the body to be finely clothed while the head is crowned with thorns.) Dress yourself as you need to, modestly, at a moderate cost, and you will please God very much. Also, as far as you can, see that your wife and sons do the same. In that way, you will be an example and a teacher for them, as a father should be, since his duty is to educate his children both with words and with virtuous deeds.

I will add one more thing: that you remain in the married state, and with fear of God treat your marriage with reverence as a sacrament, and not with improper desires. Be respectful of the days specified by the Church as a reasonable man, and not a brute animal. Then from you and your wife, as from good trees, will come forth good fruits.

If you avoid seeking public office, you will do well, for rarely does anyone fail to give offense in them. You should find even the mention of them tiring. Let the dead, then, bury themselves (see Mt 8:22). You, instead, should make every effort in freedom of heart to please God, and, in the pursuit of virtue, to love him above everything and your neighbor as yourself, fleeing the world and its delights.

— Excerpt from an undated letter written to
Messer Ristoro Canigiani, a pious layman of Florence

XII

Put on Jesus Christ

Unless the LORD builds the house,
  those who build it labor in vain.
Unless the LORD guards the city,
  the guard keeps watch in vain (Ps 127:1–2).

You see, my dear brothers and lords, that self-love ruins the city of the soul and ruins, as well as conquers, the cities of this world. I want you to also know that the world has been divided into so many groups of peoples by self-love, which also gives birth to injustice.

It seems that you desire to enhance and protect your own city, dearest brothers. This desire has inspired you to write to me, poor, miserable person that I am, so full of faults. I both listened attentively to your letter, and read it lovingly. I certainly hope that I can satisfy your request, and I will certainly exert myself, with God's grace, to pray continually for your intention. If you act in justice and conduct your government business as I have suggested, without bitter argument, selfishness, or self-interest, but for the common good and built on Jesus Christ the rock, and conduct all your business in fear of him, your prayers will preserve your city with strength, peace, and unity. Even though you have the help of the prayers of God's good servants, there is no other remedy but through love for Christ crucified. So I beg you do not drop your part of the bargain. Although you do have the help of those prayers, if you let down your guard and fail on your part to help yourselves, all will flounder.

. . . You must clothe yourselves with the New Man, sweet Jesus Christ and his immense charity. For this to happen, however, we must first be divested of self. But I will not do this unless I understand how harmful it is to cling to sin, and how very useful are these new clothes of divine love. When one witnesses his own sin, he will despise it and quickly rip it off. He will then love and dress himself up in new clothes of virtue created by love of the New Man. This is the Way. Because of this I told you of my desire to see you divested of the old man and clothed with

the New Man, Christ crucified. This is how you will pre-
vail, remain in the state of grace, and preserve your city.
You will also not fail to reverence the Holy Church.

— Excerpt from an undated letter written to
the elders and councilors of Bologna

XIII

The Soul Makes Four Requests

Inspired by a great desire for God's glory and the good of others, having spent some time learning virtue and savoring God's favor privately through self-knowledge, the soul arises, now full of love and anxious to seek truth and be clothed in it. To receive this enlightenment about God and herself, she realizes her need of humility and constant prayer. In truth, when one prays by following the footsteps of Christ crucified, that soul is united with God and he makes it another self because of its desire, affection, and love. This appears to be what Christ meant by saying: *To those who love me and observe my word, I will make myself*

known and they will be one with me and I will be one with them
(see Jn 14:21–23). There are similar words in other places
which illustrate that it really is by love that a soul becomes
his other self. If I can make this even clearer, I recall being
told by a certain servant of God how she had been in
prayer, her mind elevated to God, and God revealed to her
inner vision the love he has for his servants, saying for one
thing: "Open your inner eye and gaze into me. See the dignity and the beauty of my intelligent creatures. I have
given much beauty to the soul created in my image and
likeness. You can see those united with me in love are
clothed in the wedding garments of charity and adorned
with many virtues. Who are they, you ask me?" The sweet
loving Word responds: "These who have given up their
own wills are as another me. They are clothed with my
will, united to me, conformed to me."

Most certainly it is love that unites the soul to God.
When one sincerely wants to know the truth and follow it,
one must first lift up her own desires (knowing that a soul
can be of little use to anyone else in teaching, example, or
prayer, if she has not first mastered them personally), then
turning to the gracious, eternal Father she asks these four
petitions: first for herself; second for the reformation of
Holy Church; third for the world in general, especially
peace for those Christians who are disrespectfully in

rebellion, persecuting the Church; and fourth, that Divine Providence would take care of everything, but especially for a particular need.

— Excerpt from *The Dialogue*, Number 1 (Catherine speaks to God)

XIV

The Needs of the World Increase Our Desires

This great desire grew continuously as the awareness of the needs of the world and the whirlwind of offense toward God was shown to her by the First Truth. A letter from her spiritual father in which he lamented the suffering and intense pain caused by these offenses against God, the loss of souls, and the persecution of the Church intensified her feelings. A burning desire arose, along with sorrow for the offenses, as well as the joyful hope in anticipation of all that she imagined God would do against this evil. When receiving Communion, her soul seemed to be bound more sweetly to God, with a greater understanding of his truth (the soul is in God and God in the soul, just as a fish is in the sea, and the sea in the fish) and so she looked forward to the arrival of morning on this feast of Mary in order to hear Mass. That morning at the hour for Mass, she quickly sat in her usual place, thinking deeply of the shame of her own imperfection and that she was the reason for all the evil present in the world. Because of this, she had a certain hatred and displeasure with herself, thinking that with this self-knowledge, hatred, and a sort of holy justice, she could wash away all the impurity that seemed like a mantle of guilt on her soul. She prayed: "O eternal Father, standing before you I accuse myself so that you may punish my sins in this life. If they are the cause of the sufferings that afflict my neighbor, I beg you, please, punish me for them."

— Excerpt from *The Dialogue*, Number 2 (Catherine speaks to God)

XV

Works Require Love

"Understand that not every pain suffered in this life is a punishment; some are corrections of a son when he offends. It is true, however, that we can make satisfaction with our soul's desire, that is, not by means of the pain suffered, but with a true contrition and a detachment from sin. God, who is infinite, desires infinite love and infinite sorrow. I desire this infinite sorrow of my creature in two ways: first, by the sorrow for the sins she herself has committed against me her Creator; and secondly, by her sorrow at the sins she sees her neighbors commit against me. This infinite desire is joined to me by heartfelt charity;

they grieve when they offend me, or when they see others offend me. All their pain, whether spiritual or bodily, will receive infinite merit, and make satisfaction for guilt that deserves infinite punishment. Although their works are finite and are carried out in this finite world, their suffering is considered worthy because of their desire and because their suffering is sustained by that desire and by contrition, as well as by infinite remorse for their own guilt.

"Paul explained this: If I speak in the tongues of mortals and of angels . . . . And if I have prophetic powers, and understand all mysteries and all knowledge . . . and if I hand over my body so that I may boast, but do not have love, I gain nothing (1 Cor 13:1–3). This glorious apostle thus shows us that in themselves our finite works do not suffice for punishment or reward unless seasoned by charity."

— Excerpt from *The Dialogue*, Number 3 (God speaks to Catherine)

XVI

The Role of Desire and Contrition

"Dearest daughter, I have shown you that in this lifetime atonement is not made by any pain endured for its own sake, but by the pain endured with desire, love, and contrition. I repeat, not by virtue of the pain itself, but because of the soul's desire. Desire has value and so does every virtue. They possess life through my only-begotten Son, Christ crucified.

"From him the soul draws her love and carefully follows his virtues, that is, his footprints. There is no other way in which pain has value. Also in this way pains make up for faults because of the sweet and intimate love acquired in knowing my goodness, as well as in the bitterness and sorrow acquired by knowledge of one's self and one's own sins. In this knowledge, a hatred and displeasure with sin and one's own sensuality comes about, and it is through this that she considers herself worthy of suffering rather than of reward."

The sweet Truth continued: "See how such souls, with a contrite heart, together with love of true patience, and with true humility, considering themselves worthy of pain and unworthy of reward, await those satisfactions.

"You ask me to give you sufferings so that I may receive satisfaction for the offenses done against me by my creatures. You also ask the will to know and love me, who am the supreme Truth. My answer is that in order to find in me, the eternal Truth, perfect knowledge and pleasure, never flee from self-knowledge, for it is by humbling yourself in this lowly valley that you will know me and yourself, and from that knowledge you will draw all that is necessary. No virtue, my daughter, can have life in itself, but only in charity and in humility, the foster-mother and nurse of charity. Knowing yourself, you will humble yourself. You will see that on your own you do not even exist; your life itself comes from me. Before you existed I loved you and all others into life. In that same love I wanted to recreate you by grace, so I washed you and bathed you in the blood of my only-begotten Son, which was poured out in such a fire of love.

"Therefore, you and my other servants should conduct yourselves with true patience, with sorrow for your sins, and a love of virtue for the glory and praise of my name. I will then satisfy for all your sins, for the pains you will endure through love will be sufficient for both satisfaction and reward for you and for others. You will receive the fruit of life once your ignorance has been removed, and I will no longer remember that you offended me. Your love and affection for me will also satisfy for others. I will give them whatever they can receive of my gifts. I will especially be generous to those who listen to the teaching of my servants with humility and reverence; to them I will give true knowledge and contrition for their sins. Through prayer and their desire to serve me, they will humbly receive the fruit of grace according to the virtue they practice. Because of your intercession, their sins will be remitted. The condition, however, will be that they not be despairing because of obstinacy, in contempt of the blood that has so sweetly restored them.

"What fruit do they receive? The fruit I plan for them, suggested by my servants' intercession, is this: that I enlighten them, awaken their consciences, draw them to the perfume of virtue, entice them to joyful conversation with my servants. I may at times allow them to feel drawn by various passions so that they will be aware of what the world really is. They will seek what is above as their native country, namely, eternal life. The eye cannot see, nor the tongue adequately speak, nor the heart contemplate the number of paths or the ways by which I will lovingly lead them back to my grace so that my truth may take hold of them (see 1 Cor 2:9). My own immeasurable love for them causes me to do this, that love by which I created them, as well as the love, desire, and sorrow of my servants, because I despise neither tears, nor effort, nor humble prayer. But because I myself give them this love for souls and sorrow for their loss, I accept these gifts.

"Generally I do not allow these souls, for whom others pray, to receive any kind of relief for the punishment they have coming, but only the remission of the guilt of sin. This is because personally they are not disposed to receive my love, nor that of my servants, with perfect love. They do not sorrow bitterly, nor possess perfect contrition for the sins they committed. Theirs is imperfect love and sorrow, and so they do not receive remission of the punishment, but only of the guilt. Both the one who gives and the one who receives must be properly disposed. And so, since they are imperfect, they can only receive imperfectly from all the perfection of those who have offered their own sufferings to me for their sakes. In truth, as I told you, they only receive the remission of their sins, and then with the enlightening of the conscience and by other means, little by little they begin to understand and they spit out the vileness of their sins. Thus satisfaction is made for their guilt, and grace is received.

"These souls only know a very simple form of love. If they welcome as correction that which they receive and do not resist the mercy of the Holy Spirit, they will escape the sin and receive the life of grace. But if they foolishly show themselves to be ungrateful, ignoring me and those servants who have been laboring for them, the mercy given will become their ruin and judgment, not because of any fault in the one who begged mercy for them, but only because of their own misery and hardness of heart. This one has bound the hands of his own free will and placed a shield, hard as a diamond, over his heart, which can be smashed by nothing less than the blood. I tell you, however, that despite his hard heart, he can freely pray for the blood of my Son, while there is still time, and apply it to his diamond shield to melt it. Then he will receive the new shield of the blood that has paid his ransom. If he delays too long, there will be no remedy because he will have squandered the dowry I gave him: that is, memory by which to recall my many benefits, intelligence to see and recognize the truth, and affection to love me, the eternal Truth."

— Excerpt from *The Dialogue*, Number 4
(God speaks to Catherine)

XVII

God Is Pleased by the Desire to Suffer for Him

"To willingly endure pain and fatigue, even to the point of dying for the salvation of souls, pleases me very much. The more the soul bears, the more love it shows me. By loving me, that soul will know more of my truth, and the more it knows, the more it will suffer because of the offenses committed against me.

"You asked for my support and to let you suffer for the faults of others, unaware that what you were asking for was love, light, and a greater knowledge of the truth. I told you, however, that pain and suffering increase as love grows. Ask, therefore, and it will be given to you. I will deny nothing to one who asks with trust. Imagine that love of divine charity and perfect patience are so connected in the soul that when one is missing, so is the other. Because this is true, if one chooses to love me, they must also choose the pains I send them. Patience can only be proved in suffering; and as I have told you, patience and love are one. Therefore, be courageous. There is no other way to prove that you are spouses of my truth and faithful children who delight in my honor and in the salvation of souls."

— Excerpt from *The Dialogue*, Number 5
(God speaks to Catherine)

XVIII

Our Neighbor Affects
Our Virtues and Defects

"I would like you to realize that every virtue you have comes by means of your neighbor, every defect also. Therefore, anyone who hates me hurts his neighbor, as well as himself, since we are our own closest neighbor. It is both a general and a particular injury that is inflicted: general, because our duty is to love neighbor as self, which includes the spiritual help of prayer, the counsel of our words, and spiritual and material assistance according to his need. And if in no other way, we must at least offer him our goodwill. If you do not love me, you do not love him; if you do not love him, you do not serve him. Therefore, one who does not love, offers no help, and so injures himself. In this way, you cut yourself off from grace, and also injure your neighbors by depriving them of the good they would receive from the prayers and holy desires you would be offering to me for them. Everything, then, must be done in charity which is derived from love of me.

"Every evil is also done by means of your neighbor, for if you do not love me, you cannot love your neighbor. All evil stems from the soul's failure to love me and one's neighbor. And it follows that this person will do no good, but will in fact do evil. To whom? To one's self, first of all, and then to neighbors. But not against me, because evil cannot touch me, except that what is done to another is done to me. These people actually harm themselves by depriving themselves of grace. Nothing more harmful can be done to one's neighbor. The harm done is in avoiding payment of the debt of love and prayer and holy desire owed me for their sakes. This same assistance is owed to every person, but especially to those constantly before us, particularly to offer a word or teaching, some good example or good work, or whatever else goodness inspires. If good advice is given, counsel as you would like to be counseled, humbly and calmly. Whoever does not do this is deprived of love of neighbor and might, in fact, actually harm the neighbor because of the love not shown."

— Excerpt from *The Dialogue*, Number 6
(God speaks to Catherine).

XIX

Virtues Are Accomplished
Through Our Neighbor

"Self-love destroys charity and affection toward one's neighbor. It is the principle and foundation of every evil. All scandals, hatred, cruelty, and trouble come forth from the evil root of self-love, which has poisoned the whole world and weakened the Church's Mystical Body, as well as the entire body of Christian believers. Therefore, as I told you, it is the neighbor, that is to say the love of neighbor, that is the foundation of all virtues. Indeed that charity gives life to all the virtues, since it is impossible to obtain any virtue without charity, for charity is the pure love of me.

"This is the only way to proceed, because love of me and love of neighbor are truly one and the same thing: If one loves me, the neighbor is also loved because love of neighbor comes from me. You can see, therefore, that this is the way I have chosen for you to prove your virtue. There is nothing that you can do that will profit me and so you must do these things for your neighbor. You show that you possess me by what you do for your neighbor, as well as by your prayers in which you work diligently and lovingly for my glory and for the salvation of souls. The lover of my truth constantly serves everyone according to their need and according to their fervor. Suffering by itself cannot make up for sin; holy desire is also needed.

"You realize the usefulness of that love by which you are united with me, through which you love yourself and, at the same time, desire the salvation of the whole world. Wishing to meet the world's needs, you use the same virtue by which you reached a holy life to deal with the various needs of others. So, having seen in this love the condition of all people in general, you turn your attention to the needs of those individuals near at hand, using the graces given for this ministry: One person is helped with doctrine, that is, through words, without any show of human respect; another is helped by good example, which, of course, everyone can give by living a holy and honest life.

"These are the virtues, along with many others, too many to list, that come from love of neighbor. I have pointed them out in this way and not assigned them all to one person, but instead have given one virtue here, and another there. Nevertheless, in truth it is impossible to possess only one without having them all, since all these virtues are bound together. But among the many, there will be one that is like the head of the others. In other words, to one person I will give principally charity, to another justice, to another humility, to another lively faith, to others prudence, temperance, or patience, and to others fortitude. These virtues, and many others, I have put in my creatures in different degrees. And so, that particular virtue that is placed in a soul can be identified as its principal virtue, and the soul makes it the center of everything, through it all other virtues are attained. All virtues are bound together in love, as are the many gifts and graces resulting from virtue, and not simply in the spiritual realm, but also in the temporal. I am using the term temporal in reference to all necessities of the physical life of mankind. I have given these with total indifference, not placing them all in one soul so that individually persons would have to exercise a certain love for all other persons. It would have been easy to create a person who possessed everything necessary for the needs of body and soul, but I want people to feel the need for one another, and that they should learn to administer the gifts and graces they have received from me. And so, whether one wants to or not, no one can avoid acting in love. However, any act not made through love of me, profits nothing in the area of grace. Observe then, that I have made each person my minister and placed them in a variety of positions and ranks, so that they can practice the virtue of love.

"You see that in my house there are many mansions (see Jn 14:2), and there is nothing that I desire more than love. In loving me, one fulfills love of neighbor and observes the law. And you can only be of service in your state of life if you bind yourself to me in this love."

— Excerpt from *The Dialogue*, Number 7
(God speaks to Catherine)

XX

Virtues Proved and Fortified

"It is also true that one proves humility through a proud man, faith through the unbeliever, genuine hope through one who despairs, justice by means of the unjust, kindness by means of the cruel, gentleness and understanding through the unreasonable. A good person produces and proves all their virtues through their neighbor, just as the evil person demonstrates all their vices. And so, you could say that humility is proved through pride in this way. One who is humble has extinguished pride, since the proud cannot harm the humble; neither can an evil person's infidelity, that is the infidelity of one who neither loves me nor hopes in me, do anything against the faith or hope of one who is faithful to me. In that faith and hope born in love of me, the believer actually strengthens and proves his love for his neighbor. My faithful servant will not abandon this one simply because he does not love me faithfully, or seek for salvation by hope in me, because my faithful one sees clearly what causes this infidelity and lack of hope. The virtue of faith is proved in these and other ways. For those who need proof, my servant offers it through himself and his neighbor, and so not even the injustice of the wicked can diminish real justice, for it is proved through the just.

"The same holds for the virtues of patience, goodness, and kindness, which show themselves in times of anger as the virtues of my servants. Their love is shown in times of envy, irritation, and hatred, as well as their desire for the salvation of souls. Let me tell you that not only do those who offer good for evil prove their virtue, but often the burning coals of love completely dispel the hatred and anger in a disturbed heart. It can be said that goodwill often replaces hatred as love and perfect patience, and actually bears the defects of the one who was angry, thus supporting him. Looking at the virtues of fortitude and perseverance, you see these virtues proved by enduring for a long time the injuries and detractions of the wicked, who, either by injuries or by flattery, try constantly to cause the good to stop following the way and the teaching of truth. The virtue of fortitude, born in the soul in the midst of all these things, perseveres well and proves itself in regard to the neighbor, as I have said. Were fortitude not able to prove itself through all these tests, it would certainly not be a serious virtue founded on truth."

— Excerpt from *The Dialogue,* Number 8
(God speaks to Catherine)

XXI

Love of Virtue and Humble Discretion

"How often penance is performed with little discretion. For example, one's heart may be entirely caught up in the penance itself, rather than on love, self-hatred, true humility, perfect patience, and the other internal virtues, such as the eager longing for my glory and the salvation of souls. These virtues are important because they witness the death of self-will and demonstrate that love is continually overcoming sensuality. This is how a person should perform penances, then, with her affection centered on the virtue of love and not on the penance itself. Penance is meant as a means to gain virtue to be used as needed, and so the person must study what is possible to her. If instead one were to set up her foundation simply on the penance, she would be poisoning her own perfection, since she does not do her penance within the light of her own self-knowledge and of my truth. She does not love what I love, nor does she hate what I hate. As a virtue, discretion is nothing more than true self-knowledge and knowledge of me. Self-knowledge has only one child, discretion, which is united to charity to produce many descendants, just as a tree puts out many branches. The life of the tree, its branches, and the root is found in the ground of humility in which it is planted. This humility is foster mother and nurse of charity, who keeps the tree in the perpetual calm of discretion. The tree would not produce the virtue of discretion or any life-giving fruit were it not planted in the virtue of humility, because humility is rooted in self-knowledge. As I have already mentioned, this prompts the soul to render to each his due immediately and with discretion. The soul thus renders praise and glory to my name by acknowledging those graces and gifts known to be from me. She credits to herself that which she sees coming from herself, realizing that she cannot even account for her own existence, attributing to me her very life and all other graces received.

"In her own eyes she seems ungrateful for so many benefits, and negligent because she has not made the most of her time or the graces received. She sees herself as deserving of suffering, as hateful and unpleasant because of her guilt. All this establishes the virtue of discretion on self-knowledge. For if humility were not present, the soul would be indiscreet.

"An indiscreet soul steals the honor due me and applies it vainly to herself. Conversely she assigns to me what is indisputably her own, that is, her sorrow and complaints, because of my mysterious working in her soul and in my other creatures. Everything about me and her neighbor is a cause of scandal to her. The prudent, on the other hand, attribute to me what is my due and accept what is due to themselves. They discharge toward their neighbor the debt of love and constant prayer. This is something each person should pay to everyone else, as well as the debt of doctrine, the example of a holy and honorable life, and willingly counseling and assisting others in their pursuit of salvation. Regardless of a person's place in society, be he a noble, a bishop, or a servant, if he possesses this virtue, whatever he does for his neighbor will be done prudently and with love. These two virtues are closely intertwined, both planted in that humble ground that comes from self-knowledge."

— Excerpt from *The Dialogue*, Number 9
(God speaks to Catherine)

XXII

Living Water

"You were all invited, generally and in particular, by my Truth, when he cried out in the Temple, saying: *'Whosoever thirsts, let him come to me and drink, for I am the fountain of the water of life'* (see Jn 4:13–14; 7:37). He did not say *'Go to the Father and drink,'* but he said *'Come to me.'* He said this because in me, the Father, there can be no pain, but in my Son there can be pain. And while you are pilgrims and wayfarers in this mortal life, you cannot be without pain. Because of sin, the earth brought forth thorns. Why did he say *'Let him come to me and drink'?* He said this because whoever follows his doctrine, whether in the most perfect way or by living out a life of common charity, finds drink, tasting the fruit of the blood, through the union of the divine nature with the human nature. And you, finding yourselves in him, also find yourselves in me, who am the tranquil sea, because I am one with him, and he with me. You are invited to the fountain of living water, the fountain of grace, and it is right that with perseverance you keep close to him who has become your bridge. Do not turn back because of any contrary wind that may arise, either of prosperity or adversity. Persevere until you find me, for I am the giver of the water of life through my only-begotten Son, who is the sweet and loving Word. And why did he say: *'I am the fountain of living water'*? He said this because he was the fountain containing me, the giver of living water through the union of the divine and the human nature. Why did he say *'Come to me and drink'*? Because you cannot pass this mortal life without pain, and in me, the Father, there can be no pain, but in him there can be pain, and therefore I made him the bridge for you. No one can come to me except by him, as he told you in the words: *'No one comes to the Father except through me'* (Jn 14:6)."

— Excerpt from *The Dialogue,* Number 53
(God speaks to Catherine)

XXIII

Signs of Imperfect Love

"If someone carries away a container that he filled at a fountain and then drinks from it, that container will soon be empty. However, if he keeps his container under the fountain, even while he drinks, it will always be full. And so, love of neighbor, whether spiritual or temporal, should be enjoyed in me, without any selfish considerations. You must love me with the same love with which I love you. Actually you cannot do this, because I have loved you without being loved first by you. All your love for me is owed to me. In this way you cannot claim it is a gift, but rather it is something you ought to do. My love for you is a grace and not something I owe you. There is no way that you can repay the love you owe me so I have placed you among your neighbors, in order that you may do for them what you cannot do to me, that is, that you may love your neighbor freely, expecting nothing in return. Whatever you do for a neighbor, I count as done for me. My Truth demonstrated this when he asked Paul, my persecutor—*'Saul, Saul, why do you persecute me?'* (Acts 9:4). He said this because Paul persecuted him in his faithful people. This love must be sincere, because with the same love you have for me, you must love your neighbor. Do you know how imperfect love is demonstrated? It is shown when the lover is pained when it seems that the object of his love does not feel the same toward him, or when the conversation of the beloved turns from him, or he feels no consolation and sees that someone else is loved more than himself. All of this shows that his love for his neighbor is still imperfect.

"At first his love was drawn from me, the fountain of all love, but then he removed his container from the water in order to drink from it. His love of his neighbor is still very weak because his love for me is imperfect; the roots of self-love have not yet been dug up. I often allow this kind of love to exist in order to help someone see their own imperfection. For the same reason I withdraw any feeling for myself from the soul, so that she may enter into the house of self-knowledge, where perfection is acquired. It is then that I return to her with more light and knowledge of my truth, in proportion to how well she slays her own will through the power of grace. And she never ceases to cultivate the vine of her soul, and to root out the thorns of evil thoughts. These she replaces with the stones of virtues, cemented together in the blood of Christ crucified, which she found as she crossed the bridge of Christ, my only-begotten Son. If you remember, I told you that it is upon the bridge, that is, upon the doctrine of my truth, that the stones, based upon the virtue of his blood, were built up. In virtue of this blood, the virtues find life."

— Excerpt from *The Dialogue*, Number 64
(God speaks to Catherine)

XXIV

Vocal Prayer Leads to Mental Prayer

"Do not imagine that the soul receives great devotion and nourishment from prayer if she only prays vocally, as many people do whose prayer consists in words, not love. They only pay attention to completing the psalms and saying many times the Lord's Prayer. Once these are finished, they seem to think of nothing further. It seems they put their devoted attention and love into mere vocal recitation, which the soul is not required to do. In this way, the person bears very little fruit and pleases me little. You might ask me if it would be better for these souls to simply abandon vocal prayer, since it appears they are not called to mental prayer; I would reply *'No.'* Advancement comes by degrees, so just as a soul is at first imperfect and afterward perfect, the same is true of her prayer. It is best to continue with vocal prayer, even if imperfectly, rather than fall into idleness. However, vocal prayers should be accompanied by mental prayer; that is, while they are recited the mind should raise up in love for me, with thoughts of one's own sinfulness and of the blood of my only-begotten Son, where the fullness of my love resides, as well as remission of sins. Then the soul will recognize her own defects as well as my goodness to her, and so remain humble. I do not want you to dwell on particular defects, but think of them in general, so that you will not contaminate your mind with memories of particular, ugly sins. I do not want the soul to dwell on her sins without also remembering the blood and the greatness of my mercy. Otherwise I fear she will be confused. And with that confusion comes the devil, who actually caused the confusion under pretense of contrition and displeasure. This could lead her to eternal damnation, not just through confusion, but also through the despair she would feel at not clinging to my mercy. This is one of the subtle ways in which the devil tricks my servants. To escape this deceit and continue to please me, you must enter into my mercy and there with true humility, enlarge your heart and expand your ability to love."

— Excerpt from *The Dialogue,* Number 66
(God speaks to Catherine)

XXV

Signs of Perfect Love

"Now let me tell you how souls arrive at perfect love. They come to recognize it by the same sign given to the disciples after they received the Holy Spirit. They left the house and began to announce fearlessly the teaching of my Word, my only-begotten Son, undeterred by pain, but rather rejoicing in it. They did not mind going before this world's tyrants in order to announce the truth for the glory and praise of my name. As I have said, those who seek me through self-knowledge, receive me. I come with the fire of charity and in that charity, the soul who perseveres will bring about virtues by means of love, thus sharing in my power. It is with this power and these virtues that she overcomes and conquers her own sensitivity. Through this charity she enters into my Son's wisdom, and there with her own mind she sees and recognizes my truth, as well as the many masks of self-love. These are manifested in the imperfect love of personal consolations. She also knows the malice and lies of the devil, which he uses on those whose love is imperfect. Then the soul, awakened by a hatred of imperfection and a deep love of perfection, aligns herself with the Holy Spirit in order to strengthen her willingness to suffer pain. Coming now from her house in my name, she brings virtues to her neighbor. She does not leave that house of self-knowledge simply by coming out with virtues, however. On seeing her neighbor's need, she loses her fear of being deprived of consolation herself, and so goes ahead to birth those virtues she conceived through love."

— Excerpt from *The Dialogue*, Number 74
(God speaks to Catherine)

XXVI

Joy in the Light

"Your main thought should be to put an end to your selfishness, to neither look for nor desire anything except following my sweet Truth, Christ crucified. This is to seek only the honor and glory of my name and the salvation of souls.

"Because they live in this soothing light, they are always peaceful and calm. None of those things that normally cause scandal bother them, since they have subdued their own will. They crush underfoot all those persecutions of the world and the devil. They calmly stand in the turbulent waters of temptation. They cannot be hurt because they are anchored to the flaming branch of desire.

⟨ "Everything is joy for them. They judge neither my servants nor anyone else. Instead they find reason for joy in every situation and in every person they encounter. They say: 'Thank you, eternal Father, that in your house there are so many dwellings!' (cf. Jn 14:2). They rejoice in the great variety of ways in which people walk, more so than if all followed a similar path. In the variety they see a reflection of my goodness . . . . This is not only true of good things, but they do not pass judgment even on the sinful. Instead they are compassionate toward them. They hold them in prayer and say: 'Today this is true of you, but tomorrow it could be me if I am not sustained by grace.'"

— Excerpt from *The Dialogue*, Number 100
(God speaks to Catherine)

XXVII

The Pruning of the Perfect

"Let me say how I care for the perfect, to preserve their good effort, to prove them and help them continue on the way to greater perfection. After all, no matter how perfect one seems, that person can still be further perfected. One of the methods I employ is found in the words of my Truth, who said: 'I am the true vine, and my Father is the vinegrower. . . . you are the branches' (see Jn 15:1–5). Because he comes forth from me, the Father, he is the Truth. Whoever remains with him and believes his teachings will bear abundant fruit. In order that your fruit may increase and become perfect, I prune you with trials:

embarrassment, insults, ridicule, mistreatment, and correction, as well as hunger and thirst, both by words and by actions, in a manner that pleases me, according as each one can endure. The quality of a person's love is proven to be perfect or imperfect in such trials.

"The patience of my servant is proved during attacks and in weariness; during these, the intensity of his love will grow in accordance with his compassion for his enemy. Such a person is more moved by insults done to me or to others than insults directed at himself. This is the way of the perfect and in it they continue to grow. In fact, this is why I allow these things to happen. They may experience a burning desire for my mercy to be granted to certain souls; for this they beg constantly, taking no rest. In doing this they find that the more they forget themselves, the more they discover me."

— Excerpt from *The Dialogue*, Number 145
(God speaks to Catherine)

XXVIII

Loving Providence

" Gaze upward to me, the eternal life. Look up at the angels and those souls who are citizens of the everlasting life won for you by the blood of the Lamb. It is my desire that the reward not be enjoyed alone. You must share my gift with others. This is my will for you. Charity finds perfection and is well-ordered when it is shared: The greater rejoice in the lesser, and the least find their joy in the great. When I speak of the lesser, I refer to their capacity, because each is as full as the other. This I told you in another place, that each one has a measure all its own.

"Charity is so unique yet shared! Imagine the unity of these souls with me and with one another. I am the source of all things; they know and acknowledge this with reverent fear. They are immersed in me and within me they find their dignity. Angels converse with humans, that is, with the blessed souls, and the blessed converse with the angels. Each and all lovingly rejoice in the others' reward and jubilantly praise me without any sadness, sweetly, without any bitterness. This is so because during their lifetimes they enjoyed me in the love they shared with their neighbors. How did this come to be? It was done in my wisdom, through gentle, loving providence.

"Now look at purgatory and you will see my provident care at work for the poor foolish souls who wasted their time during life and now, separated from their bodies, can no longer depend on time. And so, I provide for their need through you who are still in the earthly life. You can do this by almsgiving, by having my ministers say the Divine Office for them, by fasting and by prayers said in the state of grace. By these means you assure that I will have mercy on these suffering souls. What gracious providence!

"I have shared with you this story of the soul's interior life and salvation, so that you will be overcome with love for my providential care and willingly clothe yourselves with the light of faith and the firmness of hope. In this way you will be freed of all selfishness and in everything you do; your trust in me will be free and assured."

— Excerpt from *The Dialogue*, Number 148
(God speaks to Catherine)

XXIX

The Vision of Eternal Life

"Throughout his life, the obedient man speaks words of peace, and at his death he receives what was promised him: eternal life, the vision of peace, and an exalted and enduring restfulness, the inestimable good that is immeasurable. Simply because it is infinite good, it cannot be understood by anything smaller than itself, somewhat like a bucket that, when dipped into the ocean, does not see the whole ocean but only the amount that it can hold. The ocean alone contains itself. So I alone, the tranquil sea, am able truly to comprehend and evaluate myself. And I rejoice in my estimation and comprehension of myself. It is this joy, this good that I have in myself, that I share with you and with everyone, according to each one's ability. I do not leave you empty, but I fill you with perfect beatitude. Each individual knows and understands my goodness in the measure that is given. And so the obedient man, possessing the light of faith in the truth that burns in the furnace of charity, anointed with humility, inebriated with the blood, accompanied by his sister patience, and with self-contempt, fortitude, perseverance, and every other virtue (that is to say, with the fruit of virtue), receives his end from me, his Creator."

— Excerpt from *The Dialogue*, Number 165
(God speaks to Catherine)

XXX

Saint Catherine's Prayer
for the Whole World
and the Holy Church

This soul, seeing by the light of faith the truth and excellence of obedience, and lovingly hearing and tasting it with an ecstatic desire, turns gratefully toward God's majesty, saying, "Thank you, eternal Father, for not despising me, the work of your hands, for not turning your face from me, nor disregarding my desires. You, pure light, have not paid attention to my darkness. You, true life, have not shunned my living death. You, the physician, have not been repulsed by my serious illness. You, eternal purity, have not paid attention to my miserable state. You, the infinite, have not considered that I am finite. You, eternal wisdom, have not seen my foolishness.

"Your wisdom, goodness, and mercy have simply overlooked my many faults and sins. Because of your merciful forgiveness, I have made your charity and love of neighbor my own. Have I been coerced? Not by my own virtues, but by your love. I pray that that same love will cause you to enlighten my mind with the light of faith, so that I may know and understand the truth you have shown me. May I remember your blessings, that I may burn with the fire of your love. May that fire inspire me to give my own body and blood, together with your blood, and then through obedience let me unlock the gate of heaven. With all my heart I beg this same blessing on everyone who makes up the Mystical Body of Christ. I believe and will never deny that you loved me before I was born. Your love is beyond description; it is as if you were madly in love with your own creature.

"Eternal Trinity! Blessed God! God who gave such value to your Son's blood, You are as deep as the sea. The deeper I dive the more I discover, and the more I discover the more I desire to find. It is impossible for a soul to be satisfied, for you are an abyss. The soul hungers for you, eternal Trinity. She desires to be able to see you with your own light. Just as a deer longs for a spring of life-giving water, so my soul desires to be liberated from the body's dark prison to actually see you. O fire and abyss of love, eternal Trinity, how long will your face be hidden from me? Quickly dispel the cloud from my body. You have given me knowledge of your truth, which pushes me to escape the weight of my body, to offer my life for your glory and praise. I have tasted, I have glimpsed your depths with the light of my mind. By your light I see you, the eternal Trinity, and the beauty of your creature. Looking at myself in you, I see that I am your image; my life is a gift of your power, O eternal Father; the wisdom of your only-begotten Son shines in my intellect and my will; from your Holy Spirit, who proceeds in oneness from you and your Son, I am able to love you. Eternal Trinity, you are my Creator; I am the work of your hands. Because of the new creation given me through your Son's blood, I know that you love what you have made.

"O profound depths! O eternal Godhead! More than yourself, what could you give me? You are the unquench-able fire, never consumed, but consuming all of my self-love; you are the fire that warms everything. Your light illuminates me to grasp all your truth. Light above all light, you supernaturally enlighten the eye of my intellect so that all is abundantly and perfectly clear. I see my soul alive, and I see it receive you, my true light. In the wisdom of your only-begotten Son, the Word, I have acquired wisdom by the light of faith. In this light of faith I am strong, constant, and persevering. In the light of faith I hope; do not let me falter. If not for this light, I would be walking in the dark; it shows me the road. I said, eternal Father, you have enlightened me by the light of holy faith.

"The soul relaxes in you, eternal Trinity, as in a calm sea. Because the water of this sea is not turbulent, the soul has no fear. Secrets are revealed in this sea with such sweetness that the soul finds certainty in what she believes. You have me gaze into the mirror of this water, holding it in my hand that I might see myself in it. And the reflection that I see is myself in you and you in me; your creature seen in you and yourself in me through that union you made of your Godhead and our humanity. For me the light represents you, the highest and infinite good, blessed and incomprehensible, inestimable beauty, exalted wisdom. You are the food of the angels; you have given yourself with burning love to us; you are the garment clothing our nakedness. Feed the hungry with your sweetness. You are sweet without any bitterness! Eternal Trinity, you have given me light to know the holy faith, that the marvelous truths you revealed about the path of perfection might be followed no longer in darkness, but in the light. This you have done that I might rise up from my sins and be a reflection of the good and holy life.

"Why have I not always known your truth and have not always loved it? I did not see you in the glorious light of faith. My self-love darkened my mind like a cloud until you, eternal Trinity, chased away the darkness with your light. Who can even imagine your greatness in order to give you proper thanks for gifts and benefits beyond measure—which you have given to me in giving the true doctrine—such a special gift above all the ordinary gifts you give to everyone? You have graciously reached down to my neediness. You allowed me to question you, and then answered in a way that satisfied my desire. You filled me with the light of grace, enough that I might duly thank you. Now clothe me, clothe me with yourself, eternal Truth, so that I may finish my life's journey in true obedience and in the light of holy faith, which makes my soul feel inebriated anew. Thanks be to God. Amen."

— Excerpt from *The Dialogue*, Number 167
(Catherine speaks to God)

Notes

1. This same evening in 1367, her "mystical marriage" to Jesus took place in the presence of Mary, John the Evangelist, Paul the Apostle, and the prophet David. She received a ring visible only to herself, and a pledge of eternal espousals.

2. This third order derived from a group of laymen gathered by Saint Dominic to reclaim properties for the Holy See. They and their wives wore black and white clothing and lived a semi-religious life. In time, the widows became The Sisters of Penance of Saint Dominic. They accepted Catherine by way of exception.

3. Gregory was succeeded by Urban VI in 1378. Immediately, the French cardinals elected a second pope, Clement VII. Despite the heroic efforts of Saint Catherine to mediate what was now the Western Schism, it continued through intrigue and war until 1409, when a united council deposed the reigning popes and elected Alexander V.

4. Saint Catherine was declared a doctor of the Church by Pope Paul VI in 1970. Pope John Paul II declared her co-patroness of Europe on October 1, 1999, along with Saint Bridget of Sweden and Saint Edith Stein.

5. *The Dialogue of Catherine of Siena* contains her mystical experiences, which she dictated to her companions from 1377–1378. At times, *The Dialogue* records Catherine speaking to God; other times, it relates God's revelation to her.

Bibliography

Brophy, Don. *Catherine of Siena: A Passionate Life*. New York: BlueBridge, 2010.

Catherine of Siena. *Le Lettere di S. Caterina da Siena*. Edited by Piero Misciattelli. Six volumes. Siena: Libreria Editrice Giuntini & Bentivoglio, 1913–1922.

Catherine of Siena. *Saint Catherine of Siena as Seen in Her Letters*. Edited and translated by Vida D. Scudder. London: J.M. Dent & Sons Ltd., 1927.

Catherine of Siena. *The Dialogue of the Seraphic Virgin, Catherine of Siena*. Edited and translated by Algar Thorold. Westminster, MD: Newman Press, 1950.

Catherine of Siena. *The Dialogue*. Translated and with an introduction by Suzanne Noeffke, O.P. New York: Paulist Press, 1980.

Gardner, Edmund G. *The Road to Siena: The Essential Biography of St. Catherine*. Edited by Jon M. Sweeney. Brewster, MA: Paraclete Press, 2009.

Jorgensen, Johannes. *Saint Catherine of Siena*. Translated by Ingeborg Lund. New York: Longmans, Green and Co., 1938.

Raymond of Capua. *The Life of Catherine of Siena*. Translated by Conleth Kearns, O.P. Wilmington, DE: Michael Glazier, Inc., 1980.

Raimondo da Capua. *S. Caterina da Siena*. Translated by P. Giuseppe Tinagli, O.P. Siena: Ezio Cantagalli, 1952.

Santa Caterina da Siena. *Il libro*. Alba: Edizioni Paoline, 1975.

BOOKS & MEDIA

The Daughters of St. Paul operate book and media centers at the following addresses. Visit, call, or write the one nearest you today, or find us on the World Wide Web, www.pauline.org.

CALIFORNIA

3908 Sepulveda Blvd, Culver City, CA 90230	310-397-8676
2650 Broadway Street, Redwood City, CA 94063	650-369-4230
5945 Balboa Avenue, San Diego, CA 92111	858-565-9181

FLORIDA

145 S.W. 107th Avenue, Miami, FL 33174	305-559-6715

HAWAII

1143 Bishop Street, Honolulu, HI 96813	808-521-2731
Neighbor Islands call:	866-521-2731

ILLINOIS

172 North Michigan Avenue, Chicago, IL 60601	312-346-4228

LOUISIANA

4403 Veterans Memorial Blvd, Metairie, LA 70006	504-887-7631

MASSACHUSETTS

885 Providence Hwy, Dedham, MA 02026	781-326-5385

MISSOURI

9804 Watson Road, St. Louis, MO 63126	314-965-3512

NEW YORK

64 W. 38th Street, New York, NY 10018	212-754-1110

PENNSYLVANIA

Philadelphia—relocating	215-676-9494

SOUTH CAROLINA

243 King Street, Charleston, SC 29401	843-577-0175

VIRGINIA

1025 King Street, Alexandria, VA 22314	703-549-3806

CANADA

3022 Dufferin Street, Toronto, ON M6B 3T5	416-781-9131

¡También somos su fuente para libros,
videos y música en español!